LAND OF LIBERTY

AMERICA'S FOOD

LYNN M. STONE

Rourke
Publishing LLC
Vero Beach, Florida 32964

www.rourkepublishing.com

PHOTO CREDITS: All photos © Lynn M. Stone except p. 4 © Lisa Loucks Christenson.

Cover Photo: *Young chefs prepare a tasty meal fit for a king!*

Editor: Frank Sloan

Cover design by Nicola Stratford

Library of Congress Cataloging-in-Publication Data

Stone, Lynn M.
  America's food / Lynn M. Stone.
    p. cm. — (Land of liberty)
  Summary: Examines the wide variety of foods and recipes found in America, many of which came from other countries.
  Includes bibliographical references and index.
    ISBN 1-58952-314-8
  1. Food habits—United States—Juvenile literature. 2. United
  States—Social life and customs—Juvenile literature. [1. Food.] I. Title
  II. Series: Stone, Lynn M. Land of Liberty

GT2853.U5 S76 2002
394.1'2—dc21   200206364

Printed in the USA

w/w

Table of Contents

Americans love to eat and have a wide variety of choices!

The Food America Likes

Americans like food hot. They like it cold. They like meat and fish, vegetables and grains. They like salty food and spicy food. They like food broiled, fried, or cooked on an open flame.

Americans like Greek food, Thai food, Italian food, and French food. They like German food, Polish food, Chinese food, and Indian food. They like **soul food** and American food, such as burgers, hot dogs, and ice cream.

Many Kinds of Food

Americans' food tastes are endless! That's largely because Americans have a chance to try so many kinds of food.

American diners eat foods from all over the world, like Danish frikadeller, *a dish of meatballs and red cabbage.*

A Mexican-American chef prepares a dish of enchiladas verde.

Americans have come from many different backgrounds. And many different foods have come from these backgrounds. Americans have a huge number of food choices. Most of them are tasty, but they are not always healthy.

People and Food

Beginning in the 1500s, Europeans began settling in America. At first there were Spaniards, French, and English. Africans came to America as slaves of the English settlers.

As the years passed, Swedes, Germans, Irish, Italians, Poles, and many more Europeans poured into America. More recently, **Hispanic** and Asian people have settled in the United States.

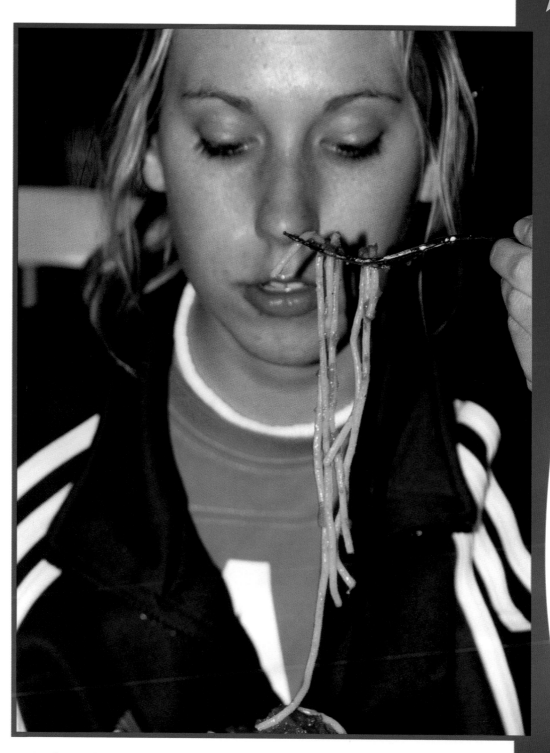

Italians brought with them to America many recipes for food dishes that use pasta noodles.

Chinese food, like this dish called Phoenix and Dragon, has become an American favorite.

Food from Many Places

Each new group that came to America brought its own recipes and food **customs**. And there was already food here. The many groups of Native Americans had a history of their own food.

It's often difficult to tell who first brought certain food dishes to America. As new groups of Americans exchanged or borrowed recipes from another group, food dishes changed. Each group tended to add its own stamp to the food it borrowed.

Hybrid Foods

Even in the early days of American history, Americans ate **hybrid** foods. The early American settlers had food with Native, English, African, European, and even Far Eastern backgrounds. Still, many food dishes in America have kept at least some of their **ethnic** character.

Once rare, Mexican restaurants have become common throughout America.

Bagels and Cream Cheese

Consider the bagel. The bagel that Eastern European Jews first brought to America was a hard roll. Pennsylvania Quakers added cream cheese to it. And today bagels are served in countless varieties.

A bagel can be served with cream cheese, raisins, berries, nuts, and other fixings.

"Foreign" Restaurants

Ethnic restaurants—Greek, Mexican, Cuban, Indian, Italian, Chinese, and many others—are everywhere in America. And each attracts Americans from all kinds of backgrounds.

The chef serves an enchilada dish that keeps its Mexican character even in America.

Tasty Italian pasta sometimes brings guests who were not invited to the table!

Ethnic Foods

Most Americans aren't afraid to try "new" foods. Many ethnic foods have become widespread in America. There are Greek gyros, German sausages, Italian pastas, and Mexican tacos and chili. Salsa, once familiar only in Mexico and the Southwest, now outsells ketchup!

The list of foods adopted in America is lengthy. There are Chinese egg rolls and stir-fried vegetables, Jewish rye bread, African chicken stew and cornbread, Japanese **tofu**, and Middle Eastern pita bread.

Stir-fried veggies (upper left and center) are part of many Chinese recipes.

A chef fills an order for Danish food.

America adopted Scandinavian herring, Danish pastries, English Yorkshire pudding, and French **soufflés**. There are, of course, many, many more.

Not So Popular

Not every dish that Americans sample becomes the next taco or spaghetti. Rattlesnake and alligator meat, for example, aren't pizza toppings yet!

Gator tail, for sale here in Florida, hasn't been a runaway seller in most of the country.

Raw whale blubber rarely leaves the plates of native Alaskan Inuit people. And the meat of **nutria**, a rodent eaten by some people in the Louisiana swamps, isn't likely to be in your next sandwich.

American tastes are wide, even daring. But the American **public** does have its limits.

Glossary

customs (CUSS tumz) — repeated practices, such as dessert after dinner

ethnic (ETH nick) — referring to a group's particular background or race, such as Indian

Hispanic (his PAN ick) — referring to people of Spanish background

hybrid (HIGH brid) — a combination of two or more; a mix of styles or dishes

nutria (NEW tree uh) — a rodent living in swamps

public (PUB lick) — the people as a whole

soufflés (soo FLAYZ) — food dishes with eggs as their main ingredient

soul food (SOLE FOOD) — traditional African American food that has its roots in slave cooking

tofu (TOH foo) — a light, almost tasteless food made of soybean curd

Index

Further Reading

Beatty, Theresa M. *Food and Recipes of Africa*. PowerKids Press, 1999.

D'Amico, Joan and Karen Drummon. *The U.S. Cookbook: Fascinating Foods and Fascinating Facts from All 50 States*. Wiley and Sons, 2000.

McCulloch, Julie. *World of Recipes: Caribbean*. Heinemann Library, 2001.

Miller, Jay. *American Indian Foods*. Children's Press, 1997.

Websites to Visit

http://library.thinkquest.org/10320/Recipes.htm

http://usatourist.com/english/inside/cooking.html

About the Author

Lynn Stone is the author of over 400 children's nonfiction books. He is a talented natural history photographer as well. Lynn, a former teacher, travels worldwide to photograph wildlife in its natural habitat.